Build a Website from Scratch

Launch Your First Website in 30 Days—Even If You've Never Written a Line of Code

Daveson Wright

Disclaimer

The information contained in this book is for general informational purposes only. While the author has made every effort to ensure that the content is accurate and up to date at the time of publication, no representations or warranties of any kind, express or implied, are made about the completeness, accuracy, reliability, suitability, or availability of the information contained within.

Any reliance you place on the information presented in this book is strictly at your own risk. The author and publisher will not be liable for any loss, injury, or damage resulting from the use of, or reliance on, the information provided.

This book is not intended as professional advice of any kind. Readers are encouraged to seek professional guidance or verify information from official sources where appropriate.

All opinions expressed in this book are those of the author and do not necessarily reflect the views of any organizations, businesses, or entities mentioned.

TABLE OF CONTENTS

CHAPTER ONE

Setting the Foundation — Understanding the Basics

Before we dive into the exciting journey of building your first website, it's important to start with a clear understanding of the basic building blocks. Don't worry—you don't need any technical background. By the end of this chapter, you'll have a strong foundation, and you'll see just how achievable creating your own website really is.

What Exactly Is a Website?

At its core, a website is simply a collection of digital pages, connected under a single domain name, that people can access through the internet. Think of it like a virtual home: each page is a different room, each with its own purpose, but all connected under one roof.

When you type a website address into your browser—like www.example.com—your computer sends a request across the internet to find that specific collection of pages. Once found, the website "unpacks" and displays the information you're looking for: articles, images, videos, stores, contact forms, and more.

Websites can be as simple as a one-page portfolio or as complex as a multi-million product online marketplace. The beauty is, you don't need a massive site to start—you just need a well-thought-out, well-built site that does exactly what you want it to do.

Whether you're creating a personal blog, a professional portfolio, a small business storefront, or a passion project, every website shares the same basic DNA. Understanding that gives you the confidence to move forward, step by step.

Domains, Hosting, and How the Internet Works

Now, let's break down three of the most important terms you'll encounter: **domain**, **hosting**, and **the internet**.

What Is a Domain?

A domain is the address where visitors find your website. It's what you type into the browser—like www.yourwebsite.com.

Think of it like the street address for your home. Without it, nobody would know how to find you.

Choosing a domain name is one of the most important steps you'll take. It should be memorable, easy to spell, and ideally hint at what your site is about. We'll go deeper into picking the perfect domain in later chapters, but for now, just know: your domain is your digital identity.

What Is Hosting?

If a domain is your address, **hosting** is the land your house sits on. Hosting providers store all the files, images, and data that make up your website. When someone visits your domain, the host serves up the right files so your website appears on their screen.

Hosting companies maintain powerful computers called **servers**. These servers are always connected to the internet and always ready to deliver your website to anyone, anywhere, anytime.

There are different types of hosting services—from basic shared hosting to powerful dedicated servers—but for most beginners, affordable and reliable shared hosting will work perfectly.

How the Internet Connects It All

Imagine the internet as a giant, sprawling network of roads and highways. Every device—your phone, laptop, or smart TV—is a vehicle driving along those roads. Domains are like billboards telling drivers where to go, while hosting servers are the buildings or destinations drivers arrive at.

Behind the scenes, a system called **DNS** (Domain Name System) acts like a traffic controller, ensuring that when someone types your domain name, they are directed to the correct server hosting your website. This all happens in milliseconds, making it feel instant to users.

Understanding how these pieces fit together—domain, hosting, and internet traffic—will help demystify the process and give you a big advantage as you start to build.

Website Types: Blog, Portfolio, E-Commerce, and Beyond

Not all websites are created for the same purpose. One of the first decisions you'll make is what *type* of website you want to build. Let's explore the most common types to help you choose the right one for your goals.

Blog

A blog is a series of articles, journal entries, or informational posts, usually organized chronologically.

Blogs are fantastic for sharing knowledge, personal experiences, or updates. Whether you're passionate about travel, food, fashion, or business tips, a blog allows you to connect with an audience through regular content updates.

Many successful online businesses started out as simple blogs. Over time, a blog can grow into a powerful platform, opening doors to opportunities like partnerships, sponsorships, and even book deals.

Portfolio

If you're a creative professional—like a photographer, graphic designer, writer, or artist—a portfolio website is your digital resume. It showcases your best work, introduces who you are, and invites potential clients or employers to reach out.

A portfolio site typically includes a clean homepage, an "About" section, galleries or project pages, and a contact form. Building a portfolio site is often the fastest path to getting your talents discovered.

E-Commerce Store

An e-commerce website lets you sell products or services directly online. From handmade crafts to digital downloads, physical products to coaching sessions, an online store opens your business to a global audience 24/7.

While setting up an e-commerce site involves a few extra steps—like payment processing and inventory management—modern tools make it easier than ever. Shopify, WooCommerce, and Squarespace Commerce are just a few platforms that allow even beginners to launch their own online shops with minimal fuss.

Business Website

Every business today, no matter how small, needs a professional online presence. A business website typically includes information about services, customer testimonials, pricing, a blog, and clear ways for visitors to get in touch or book an appointment.

Even if you're running a local service like dog walking, plumbing, or life coaching, having a simple, polished website instantly boosts credibility and trust.

Landing Page or One-Page Website

Sometimes, less is more. A landing page or single-page site focuses on one main message—like promoting a product launch, collecting email signups, or showcasing a single event. They are fast to build, easy to manage, and incredibly effective when done right.

This option is perfect if you want to start small and grow over time.

CHAPTER TWO

Planning Your Website Like a Pro

Before you dive headfirst into building your website, take a moment to step back and plan. A well-planned website is like a beautifully built house—it's sturdy, welcoming, and designed with purpose. Skipping this step is one of the most common mistakes beginners make, leading to frustration, wasted time, and websites that miss the mark.

Planning your website isn't about making things complicated—it's about giving yourself a clear roadmap. When you know where you're going, every decision becomes easier, faster, and more effective.

Let's get started.

Defining Your Purpose and Goals

Every great website starts with a simple question: **Why am I building this website?**

It may seem obvious, but you'd be surprised how often this question gets overlooked. Without a clear purpose, it's easy to end up with a scattered site that tries to do everything—and ultimately achieves nothing.

Here are some common website purposes:

- **To share knowledge or ideas** (like a blog)
- **To showcase skills and experience** (like a portfolio)
- **To sell products or services** (like an e-commerce store)
- **To generate leads for a business** (like a business site)
- **To create a community or movement** (like a membership or non-profit site)

Once you have your primary purpose nailed down, it's time to define your **goals**.

Goals are specific outcomes you want your website to achieve. They turn a broad purpose into focused action.

Here are a few examples:

- Grow an email list to 1,000 subscribers
- Sell 100 products in the first three months
- Book five client consultations each month
- Get published articles read by 10,000 people in a year

Good goals are S.M.A.R.T.:

- **Specific** – Clear and precise
- **Measurable** – You can track progress
- **Achievable** – Realistic with your resources
- **Relevant** – Aligned with your overall vision
- **Time-bound** – Attached to a deadline

By defining both your purpose and goals upfront, you create a strong compass that guides every decision you make—from design choices to the words you write.

Understanding Your Audience

After you know what you want your website to accomplish, the next step is understanding *who* you're building it for.

Your audience isn't "everyone." Trying to speak to everyone usually means speaking effectively to no one. Instead, think carefully about the specific group of people who will benefit most from your website.

Here's how to start:

Create a Simple Audience Profile

Ask yourself:

- **Who are they?** (Age, gender, occupation, interests)
- **What are they looking for?** (Information, services, products, entertainment)
- **What problems or desires do they have?** (Pain points or dreams)

- **How do they prefer to consume content?** (Short blog posts, detailed guides, videos, images)

For example, if you're creating a website for freelance graphic design services, your audience might be small business owners who need professional branding but can't afford big design agencies. They want quick, clear examples of your work, easy pricing information, and a fast way to get in touch.

Why Understanding Your Audience Matters:

- It shapes your tone of voice (formal, casual, motivational, educational)
- It determines your design choices (color schemes, layout, style)
- It influences your content (what topics you cover, how you present your offers)

When you build your website with a crystal-clear picture of your audience in mind, your site becomes like a magnet, naturally attracting the right visitors and encouraging them to take action.

Sketching Out Your Site Structure (Simple Sitemaps)

Now that you know your purpose, goals, and audience, it's time to sketch out the structure of your site.

Think of your website as a house again—before you start building walls, you need a blueprint. That blueprint is called a **sitemap**.

What Is a Sitemap?

A sitemap is a simple outline that shows how all the different pages of your website connect. It's a visual way to organize your ideas and ensure that visitors can find what they need easily.

Keep It Simple.

At this stage, you don't need a fancy tool or complicated software. A piece of paper, a whiteboard, or a basic online diagram tool will do perfectly.

Start with the basics. Here's a classic beginner-friendly sitemap structure:

1. **Home Page**
   - Brief welcome
   - Introduction to what you offer
   - Clear paths to other important sections
2. **About Page**
   - Your story or your business story
   - Mission and values
   - Why visitors should trust you
3. **Services/Products Page**
   - Detailed information about what you offer
   - Benefits and features
   - Pricing if applicable
4. **Blog (optional)**
   - Regular articles or updates to drive traffic and build authority

5. **Contact Page**
   - o Easy-to-find form, email address, or booking tool
   - o Links to social media if relevant
6. **FAQs/Testimonial Page (optional)**
   - o Address common questions
   - o Build trust with client/customer testimonials

Tips for Great Site Structure:

- **Keep it simple and intuitive.** Visitors should find what they're looking for without thinking too hard.
- **Prioritize clarity over creativity.** Clever menu names sound fun but can confuse visitors. Use straightforward labels like "About," "Services," and "Contact."
- **Limit the number of main menu items.** Around 4–6 top-level items is a good target to avoid overwhelming your visitors.

CHAPTER THREE

Choosing the Right Tools — No Coding Needed

The beauty of building a website today is that you don't have to be a coding wizard to create something stunning, functional, and professional. Thanks to modern website-building tools, anyone—from complete beginners to tech-savvy entrepreneurs—can bring their vision to life.

However, with so many options available, choosing the right platform can feel overwhelming. Should you use a website builder? Should you dive into WordPress? Which tool truly fits your needs?

In this chapter, we'll break it down clearly and simply, so you can confidently choose the right tools to get your website off the ground.

Website Builders vs. WordPress: Which One Fits You?

When you start exploring how to build a website without coding, you'll quickly encounter two main paths: **Website Builders** and **WordPress**.

Each has its strengths and weaknesses. Understanding them will help you choose the one that's best for your project.

Website Builders: The All-in-One Solution

Website builders like Wix, Squarespace, and Shopify are designed to be as user-friendly as possible. They offer:

- **Drag-and-drop interfaces** (move elements around easily)
- **Pre-designed templates** (beautiful designs ready to customize)
- **Built-in hosting** (no need to purchase separate hosting)
- **Integrated support** (help when you need it)

Pros of Website Builders:

- Extremely easy to use, even for beginners
- Quick setup—you can have a site live in a few hours
- All-in-one packages (domain, hosting, design tools, security)

Cons of Website Builders:

- Less flexibility if you want to deeply customize
- Monthly fees can add up over time
- Limited control if you want to migrate your site later

Best for:

People who want a beautiful, functional website fast without worrying about the technical side.

WordPress: The Flexible Powerhouse

When people say "WordPress," they usually mean **WordPress.org**—a free, open-source platform that powers over 40% of all websites globally. (Note: WordPress.com is a hosted version, which we'll explain shortly.)

Pros of WordPress:

- Ultimate flexibility—you can build any kind of site
- Thousands of themes and plugins to expand functionality
- Greater control over SEO (search engine optimization)
- You fully own and control your website

Cons of WordPress:

- Slightly steeper learning curve
- You'll need separate hosting
- Requires more maintenance (like updates and backups)

Best for:

People who want complete control, scalability, and are willing to invest a little more time upfront.

Overview of Top Platforms (Wix, Squarespace, WordPress.com, Shopify)

Let's take a quick tour of some of the top website-building platforms. Each has its unique features, and one might be the perfect match for your goals.

Wix

Wix is a drag-and-drop builder known for its intuitive interface and vast range of design options. It offers hundreds of stunning templates, and you can easily customize your site with simple clicks.

Strengths:

- Very beginner-friendly
- Excellent design flexibility
- App Market for additional features

Best for:

Personal websites, small businesses, creatives, and portfolios.

Squarespace

Squarespace emphasizes elegant design and simplicity. Its templates are some of the most beautiful on the market, especially for visually-driven websites like photography portfolios or boutique stores.

Strengths:

- Gorgeous, modern templates
- All-in-one solution (domain, hosting, SSL)
- Strong blogging and e-commerce capabilities

Best for:

Artists, photographers, small businesses, and anyone who values polished aesthetics.

WordPress.com

WordPress.com is the hosted cousin of WordPress.org. It removes some of the technical headaches by managing hosting, security, and backups for you.

Strengths:

- Easy to start, with free and paid plans
- Ideal for blogs and basic websites
- Upgradeable to more powerful features

Best for:

Bloggers, writers, nonprofits, and anyone starting small but thinking big.

Shopify

Shopify is a specialized platform focused purely on e-commerce. It's the go-to choice for entrepreneurs who want to open an online store and start selling immediately.

Strengths:

- Built specifically for online selling
- Powerful inventory, shipping, and payment tools
- App Store for expanding your store's functionality

Best for:

E-commerce businesses, from startups to large-scale retailers.

Picking a Platform Based on Your Needs

Now that you have an overview, how do you choose the right platform for *your* specific situation? Here's a simple way to approach it:

1. Identify Your Primary Goal

- **Want to blog?** WordPress.com or Squarespace might suit you best.

- **Selling products?** Shopify is tailor-made for that.
- **Showcasing your portfolio?** Wix or Squarespace are great choices.
- **Want long-term flexibility?** Go with WordPress.org.

2. Consider Your Budget

Website builders usually involve a **monthly fee** that covers hosting and support. WordPress.org itself is free, but you'll need to pay for hosting, a domain name, and potentially a premium theme or plugin.

Here's a rough idea:

- Wix/Squarespace: $12–$30 per month
- WordPress.org: $5–$15 per month for hosting, plus optional extras
- Shopify: $29–$299 per month, depending on the plan

Tip: Always factor in future growth. Paying a little more for a platform that fits your future goals can save you a lot of headaches later.

3. Think About Design and Customization

- **Love creative control?** WordPress gives you endless possibilities.
- **Want a stunning design quickly?** Squarespace and Wix offer beautiful templates you can tweak easily.

4. Evaluate Your Technical Comfort Level

- If you prefer a simple, guided process without touching technical settings, go with Wix, Squarespace, or WordPress.com.
- If you're open to learning a little more, and want to customize your site deeply, WordPress.org is an excellent investment of your time.

CHAPTER FOUR

Branding Your Website

Creating a website is not just about putting content online—it's about building a brand that leaves a lasting impression. Think about the websites you visit regularly. Chances are, you remember them not just because of what they offer, but because of how they *feel*. That feeling is the power of branding at work.

Branding is the invisible thread that ties your website's purpose, design, and message together into a memorable identity. It's how you tell your story, show your personality, and build trust with visitors— all without speaking a word.

Crafting a Memorable Name

Your website's name is your first handshake with the world. It's the first thing people see, hear, and remember. A strong name sets the tone for your brand and instantly communicates something about who you are.

When crafting your website's name, think about three key factors: clarity, simplicity, and relevance.

First, **clarity** is crucial. A name should immediately give people an idea of what your site is about. If you're launching a photography portfolio, names like "Golden Lens" or "Capture Essence" tell a story before anyone even clicks.

Second, **simplicity** wins. The best website names are easy to spell, easy to say, and easy to remember. Complicated names might sound clever but can leave visitors confused—or worse, forgetting you altogether.

Third, **relevance** keeps you connected to your audience. Choose a name that resonates with the emotions or expectations of your ideal visitors. If you're building an online shop for handmade jewelry, a name like "SilverWhisper" speaks more directly than something generic like "BestCrafts123."

Tips for Crafting Your Name:

- Brainstorm a list of words related to your site's theme, values, and audience.
- Play with combinations, metaphors, and imagery.
- Say it out loud—is it pleasant to hear?
- Check domain name availability to ensure you can claim your brand online.

Remember: the right name doesn't have to be perfect from the start—it just has to be authentic to your brand and easy for people to remember.

Choosing Colors, Fonts, and Imagery

Once you have your name, it's time to start painting your website's personality through design. The colors, fonts, and images you choose create a visual language that speaks to your audience's emotions before they even read a single word.

Colors: Setting the Mood

Colors are more powerful than most people realize. They instantly trigger feelings and perceptions. Here's a quick guide to color psychology:

- **Blue** evokes trust, calm, and professionalism.
- **Red** brings energy, passion, and urgency.
- **Green** symbolizes growth, nature, and balance.
- **Yellow** radiates optimism, cheerfulness, and warmth.
- **Black** exudes sophistication and luxury.
- **White** conveys simplicity, cleanliness, and openness.

Choosing your color palette should start with asking: *What emotions do I want my visitors to feel?* A wellness blog might lean into calming greens and soft whites, while a tech startup might choose bold blues and grays.

Pro Tip:

Stick to **two or three main colors**. Too many colors can confuse and overwhelm your audience.

Fonts: Communicating Personality

Fonts might seem small, but they make a huge impact on how professional and readable your site feels. There are two main types of fonts:

- **Serif fonts** (like Times New Roman) feel traditional, trustworthy, and elegant.
- **Sans-serif fonts** (like Arial or Helvetica) feel modern, clean, and friendly.

Choosing one main font for headings and another complementary font for body text keeps your design consistent and polished. Avoid using more than two different fonts on your website—it can quickly look chaotic.

Pro Tip:

Make sure your font is easy to read across devices. Fancy fonts might look beautiful on a laptop but become illegible on a phone.

Imagery: Telling Your Story Visually

Images are the quickest way to tell your brand's story. Authentic, high-quality visuals instantly make a website feel more professional and relatable. When selecting or creating images for your site:

- Choose photos that align with your brand's tone and audience.
- Use consistent filters or editing styles for a cohesive look.
- Avoid overly staged or cliché stock photos whenever possible.

If you can, incorporate custom imagery—like pictures of your products, behind-the-scenes shots, or illustrations that reflect your brand's unique personality.

Designing a Simple, Strong Logo (Even Without a Designer)

Logos are often seen as the cornerstone of a brand. They act as a visual shortcut for people to recognize and remember you. The good news? You don't need to hire an expensive designer to create a logo that works.

Here's how to create a simple, effective logo:

1. Focus on Simplicity

The best logos are simple. Think about the logos you know by heart—Nike's swoosh, Apple's apple, McDonald's golden arches. A complicated logo will shrink poorly on mobile screens and lose impact. Aim for a clean design that looks good both large and small.

2. Make It Relevant

Your logo should hint at what your brand represents. If you're starting a travel blog, maybe a small compass or globe integrated into the logo makes sense. If you're launching a bakery website, a cupcake outline might be perfect.

3. Choose the Right Tool

There are excellent free or affordable tools you can use to create a logo, even without design experience:

- **Canva** offers easy-to-use templates.
- **Looka** uses AI to generate logo options based on your style preferences.
- **Hatchful** by Shopify creates free logos tailored to your industry.

These tools allow you to customize fonts, icons, and colors until your logo feels right.

4. Think About Versatility

Your logo should look great in different contexts— on your website, your social media profiles, business cards, or even merchandise. Create versions that work in full color, black and white, and small sizes.

Pro Tip:

Save high-resolution files in different formats (PNG, SVG) so you're ready for any use.

CHAPTER FIVE

Buying Your Domain and Hosting

Bringing your website to life begins with securing its digital real estate. Just like a physical shop needs a location, your website needs a home on the internet—and that starts by purchasing your domain and hosting. These two steps may seem technical or intimidating at first glance, but they are crucial milestones in your journey from dreamer to website owner.

When you secure a domain and hosting, you claim your unique space in the vast digital landscape. It's the first act of commitment to your project.

How to Choose the Right Domain Name

A domain name is more than just an address—it's a powerful part of your brand identity. It's the word that people will type into their browsers to find you, the phrase they will say when recommending your site to a friend, and the label that will appear on business cards, advertisements, and search engine results. Choosing the right domain name is an investment in the future of your brand.

The best domain names are simple, memorable, and meaningful. They act as a bridge between the essence of your website and the people you hope to reach. A great domain name captures the spirit of your project and plants it firmly in the minds of visitors. In many ways, it's your website's first impression—and you want it to be a lasting one.

Ideally, your domain should closely match the name of your website or business. Consistency is crucial because it reduces confusion and makes it easier for people to remember you. Shorter names are often better; they are easier to type and less prone to mistakes.

If possible, avoid hyphens and complicated spellings, as they can disrupt the flow and make your site harder to find.

Another important factor is the domain extension you choose. The ".com" extension is the gold standard because it is universally recognized and trusted.

However, depending on your niche, you might consider other options like ".net," ".org," or industry-specific extensions like ".design" or ".store." Still, if ".com" is available, it's usually wise to secure it.

Above all, a great domain name should feel natural when spoken aloud. If it feels awkward to say, it will feel awkward to type and remember. Try saying your potential names to friends or colleagues. Their immediate reactions will give you valuable clues about how the name will be received by a broader audience.

Finding a Reliable Hosting Provider

Once you have a domain name in mind, the next step is to find a hosting provider—a company that will store your website's files and make them accessible to people around the world. Think of hosting as renting space on a server where your website will live.

Not all hosting providers are created equal. Choosing the right one can make the difference between a smooth, professional experience and one filled with technical headaches. Speed, reliability, customer support, and scalability are all key considerations when evaluating hosting services.

Speed matters because visitors expect websites to load quickly. If your hosting service is slow, it can lead to frustrated visitors who leave before they ever explore your content.

Search engines like Google also take website speed into account when ranking sites, meaning a sluggish host can hurt your visibility online.

Reliability is equally important. You want your website to be available 24/7. Look for hosting providers that guarantee at least 99.9% uptime. Anything less could result in lost opportunities and a tarnished reputation.

Customer support can be a lifesaver, especially when you're starting out. At some point, you might encounter a technical issue or have questions you can't answer on your own. A hosting provider with responsive, knowledgeable support staff can turn a stressful situation into a minor inconvenience.

Lastly, think about scalability. While your website might start small, your goal is for it to grow. Choosing a hosting provider that offers flexible plans allows you to expand seamlessly as your traffic increases.

When selecting a provider, take time to read reviews, explore the features they offer, and understand their pricing structure. Some well-known names in the hosting world include Bluehost, SiteGround, and HostGator, but there are many excellent options depending on your specific needs.

Step-by-Step Guide to Registering Your Domain and Setting Up Hosting

Once you have selected your domain name and hosting provider, it's time to officially claim your space on the internet. The process is straightforward, and with a little guidance, it can even be enjoyable— a clear signal that your dream is becoming real.

The journey usually begins on your chosen hosting provider's website. Most reputable hosts also offer domain registration, allowing you to bundle both services together for simplicity and potential discounts.

Once on the site, you'll use a search bar to check if your desired domain name is available. If it's taken, the system will often suggest alternatives, or you may need to brainstorm a slight variation that keeps the spirit of your original idea.

After securing an available domain, you will proceed to create an account with the hosting provider. During this step, you will choose a hosting plan.

Many providers offer tiers based on features and the expected volume of website visitors. For a first website, a basic shared hosting plan is often sufficient—and it's the most budget-friendly choice. However, if you expect rapid growth or need specific technical features, exploring higher-tier plans may be worthwhile.

During checkout, you may encounter add-ons such as privacy protection, which hides your personal information from public domain records, or automated backup services, which safeguard your site's content.

While not always essential, these extras can provide valuable peace of mind, especially as you get your feet wet in the world of website ownership.

Once your domain and hosting are purchased, you'll usually have access to a dashboard where you can manage your new site. Many hosting providers offer a "one-click install" for platforms like WordPress, allowing you to set up a functioning website foundation with just a few clicks. From there, you can begin customizing your site, adding content, and bringing your vision to life.

Setting up hosting also involves connecting your domain name to your server. In many cases, if you purchase both from the same provider, this connection is handled automatically.

If they are separate, you will need to point your domain's name servers to your hosting account—a task that sounds technical but is simple when following your host's step-by-step instructions.

At the end of this process, you will have something tangible: your domain will exist online, tied to a space where your website will live and grow.

It's a thrilling moment—the digital equivalent of putting up a sign on the door of your new venture, ready to welcome visitors from around the world.

CHAPTER SIX

Building Your Website Step-by-Step

The foundation has been laid. You have a domain name secured, a reliable hosting provider in place, and a vision for what you want to create. Now comes one of the most exciting parts of the journey—actually building your website. Though it may seem like a daunting task, it becomes surprisingly approachable when broken down into clear, manageable steps.

This chapter will walk you through installing your platform, choosing a design template that matches your brand, and setting up the essential pages that will serve as the backbone of your site.

The beauty of today's digital tools is that you no longer need to know how to code to build a professional, impressive website. Whether you choose WordPress, Wix, or another platform, the path forward is designed to be intuitive and empowering.

Every step you take brings you closer to launching a site that represents you, your business, or your project to the world.

Installing Your Platform

Your hosting account and domain name have created a space for your website, but it is your chosen platform that will determine how you interact with it day to day.

WordPress, Wix, Squarespace, Shopify—each of these offers a different approach to website building, tailored to different needs and skill levels. Fortunately, getting your platform installed and ready is a straightforward process.

If you are using WordPress—a popular choice for its flexibility and control—most hosting providers offer a "one-click install" option. Logging into your hosting dashboard, you will typically find a button that initiates the installation. With a few simple prompts, WordPress will be installed on your domain, and you will receive login credentials for your site's administrative dashboard.

WordPress provides an immense amount of freedom; it is open-source and highly customizable, making it ideal for everything from simple blogs to complex e-commerce stores.

For those opting for Wix or Squarespace, the process is even more streamlined. These platforms are hosted solutions, meaning you sign up directly on their websites without needing a separate hosting provider.

Once you create an account, you will be guided through an onboarding process where you can choose a site type, select a template, and begin editing right away. They handle the technical side—updates, security, backups—leaving you free to focus solely on design and content.

No matter the platform you choose, the important thing is to feel comfortable. You are building something personal, something that should inspire confidence.

Taking the time to explore your dashboard, familiarize yourself with the basic settings, and understand how to navigate your platform will make the rest of your journey much smoother.

Picking and Customizing a Template

The next critical step is giving your site its visual identity, and that starts with picking a template. A template, sometimes called a theme, is the framework for your site's design. It sets the layout, style, and overall aesthetic, allowing you to create a visually cohesive site without designing every element from scratch.

Choosing a template should be a thoughtful decision. Your website's design says a lot about you at a glance—it conveys professionalism, personality, and purpose without a single word being read. Different templates are crafted with different goals in mind; some are sleek and minimalist, perfect for portfolios, while others are vibrant and dynamic, ideal for creative businesses or online stores.

When browsing templates, prioritize clarity and usability over flashy animations or complicated structures. A clean, intuitive design ensures that visitors can easily navigate your site, find the information they need, and have a positive experience. Remember, form follows function. A beautiful site that is difficult to use will ultimately fail its visitors.

Once you have selected a template that resonates with your brand, customization begins. Templates serve as starting points, but personalization brings them to life. Modify the colors to match your brand palette, choose fonts that align with your voice, and replace default images with photos that reflect your message.

Most platforms make these adjustments as simple as clicking and dragging, making it easy even for beginners to create something uniquely theirs.

Resist the temptation to overcomplicate. Keep your design consistent across all pages, use a restrained color scheme, and make sure that your fonts are readable across devices. Your goal is to create a welcoming environment that draws visitors in and encourages them to stay.

Setting Up Essential Pages

As your site's look and feel take shape, the next step is setting up its core structure: the essential pages that every website needs. These pages provide visitors with the information they expect and establish the foundation for deeper engagement.

The Home page is your front door, the first impression most visitors will have. It should clearly communicate who you are, what you offer, and invite visitors to explore further.

A strong Home page balances eye-catching visuals with concise, compelling text. It guides visitors toward the next steps you want them to take, whether that's reading more, viewing products, or contacting you.

The About page provides an opportunity to share your story. People connect with people, not faceless brands, and the About page is your chance to establish that human connection. Tell visitors who you are, what drives you, and why you created your website. Authenticity wins trust, and trust forms the foundation of any lasting relationship.

A Services or Products page (depending on your site's purpose) lays out what you offer. Here, clarity is key. Clearly describe each service or product, outline the benefits, and make it easy for visitors to understand how to engage with you. Strong calls to action—encouraging visitors to book, buy, or learn more—make these pages truly effective.

Finally, the Contact page ensures that visitors have an easy way to reach you. Whether you include a simple form, an email address, a phone number, or links to social media, the important thing is to make communication effortless.

You might also consider embedding a map if you have a physical location, or including office hours if you expect inquiries by phone.

Creating these essential pages provides structure and focus to your website. It also establishes credibility—visitors expect these pages, and their absence can create unease.

With these in place, your site will feel complete, even as you continue to add new content and features over time.

CHAPTER SEVEN

Creating Compelling Content

Your website is nearly ready to go live, but there's one final critical piece that will make it truly stand out: compelling content. A website without strong, engaging content is like a beautiful building with no interior—people may stop by to admire its exterior, but they won't stick around for long. Content is what drives engagement, builds trust, and ultimately converts visitors into customers, followers, or subscribers.

In this chapter, we will dive into the essentials of creating website content that connects with your audience and sparks action. We'll cover how to write website copy that converts, the best practices for using images and videos to enhance your message, and how adding a blog can boost your site's impact.

Each of these elements plays an essential role in making your website a powerful tool for building relationships and achieving your goals.

Writing Website Copy That Converts

When visitors land on your website, you have just a few seconds to grab their attention. If your copy doesn't immediately communicate value, they'll move on.

Crafting persuasive, clear, and concise copy is a skill that requires both creativity and strategic thinking. Your goal is to compel visitors to take action— whether that means purchasing a product, subscribing to a newsletter, or simply exploring more of your site.

Start by defining the core message you want to communicate on each page. What is the purpose of this page, and what do you want the visitor to do next? Your copy should clearly answer those questions.

For example, on a product page, the message could be: "This product will solve your problem" or "Experience the difference with our innovative solution." This simple clarity builds trust and gives the visitor a reason to continue engaging.

In addition to being clear, your copy should be customer-centric. People don't come to your website to read about how great you are—they come to find out how you can help them.

Focus on the benefits of your services or products, not just the features. Tell your audience how your offering can solve a problem, improve their life, or make their day easier. Using a "you" perspective—speaking directly to your visitors—helps them feel like the content is personally relevant to them.

Using strong calls to action (CTAs) is another key aspect of compelling copy. A CTA is an instruction that tells visitors what to do next. Phrases like "Buy Now," "Learn More," or "Sign Up Today" are direct and effective, but they should be tailored to your goals and tone.

Whether you're offering a free consultation, encouraging visitors to download a resource, or prompting them to subscribe to your blog, the CTA should be clear, easy to follow, and action-oriented.

Finally, make sure your copy is easy to scan. Online readers tend to skim content, so break up your text into short paragraphs, use bold and italics for emphasis, and incorporate bullet points where possible. This approach ensures that even if someone doesn't read every word, they'll still absorb your key messages.

Best Practices for Images and Videos

Images and videos have the power to transform your website from static text to a vibrant, interactive experience. They can evoke emotion, illustrate key points, and break up long sections of text, making your website more engaging and visually appealing.

However, to be effective, images and videos need to be carefully selected and optimized.

First, consider the purpose of each image. Is it meant to explain something, evoke a feeling, or showcase a product? For example, on a product page, high-quality images of the product from multiple angles give visitors a clear view of what they're buying.

Lifestyle images that show the product in use can also help potential customers visualize how it will fit into their lives. The right image doesn't just fill space—it reinforces the message of your copy and enhances the user experience.

When it comes to videos, the same principle applies. A well-crafted video can communicate complex ideas quickly and effectively, making it an invaluable asset on a website. Whether it's a product demo, an explainer video, or a customer testimonial, videos give your visitors a deeper connection to your brand. Just as with images, though, quality matters.

Ensure that your videos are clear, concise, and professionally produced—poor-quality videos can hurt your credibility.

Another important aspect of using images and videos is optimizing them for web performance. Large, uncompressed files can slow down your website, leading to frustrating delays for visitors.

Ensure that your media files are appropriately sized and compressed without sacrificing too much quality. Most platforms, like WordPress and Squarespace, offer plugins or built-in tools to help with image optimization.

Additionally, don't overlook accessibility. Alt text for images and captions for videos are essential for accessibility, ensuring that all visitors, including those with disabilities, can engage with your content. Alt text also improves SEO, helping search engines understand what your images represent, which can boost your visibility in search results.

Adding a Blog: Optional, but Powerful

One of the most powerful ways to enhance your website's content is by adding a blog. While it may not be necessary for every website, a blog offers tremendous value if used correctly. It's an ongoing, dynamic content source that can engage your audience, improve your SEO, and establish your authority in your field.

A blog allows you to share your expertise, insights, and updates with your audience in a format that encourages interaction and repeat visits. For businesses, it's an excellent way to keep customers informed about new products, special offers, or company news.

If you're a creative professional, a blog can showcase your work, share your creative process, and offer tips or inspiration to others in your industry. Bloggers often find that over time, their blog becomes a key tool for building a loyal, engaged community.

In terms of SEO, a blog can be a game-changer. By regularly publishing high-quality content, you create more opportunities to rank in search engines for relevant keywords.

For example, if you're running a landscaping business, writing a blog post on "How to Choose the Right Plants for Your Garden" can help your site rank for related searches. Each blog post becomes an opportunity to appear in search results, driving more organic traffic to your website.

But blogging doesn't just benefit your SEO. It also provides valuable, shareable content that can be distributed across your social media channels. Each post you publish is another piece of content that your audience can engage with, share, and discuss, further spreading the word about your website and what you offer.

However, starting a blog requires commitment. It's important to update it regularly with fresh, relevant content. While it's tempting to post sporadically, consistency is key to building an audience and reaping the full benefits of blogging. Aim to publish at least one post per month, but more frequent updates—like once a week—can yield even greater results.

CHAPTER EIGHT

Optimizing for Mobile and User Experience

In today's digital world, the experience visitors have on your website is paramount to its success. With more people accessing websites from their smartphones and tablets than ever before, ensuring your site is optimized for mobile devices is no longer optional—it's a necessity.

A website that doesn't look great or function well on mobile devices will possible lose a great portion of its potential audience. In this chapter, we will explore why mobile-first design matters, how to make your site mobile-friendly, and the role of navigation and speed in keeping visitors engaged.

Why Mobile-First Design Matters

As recently as a decade ago, desktop computers were the primary means through which people accessed the internet. However, the rise of smartphones has revolutionized web browsing.

In fact, mobile internet usage now accounts for over half of all web traffic globally. This shift has led to the concept of mobile-first design—the practice of designing websites with a mobile user experience as the priority.

The mobile-first approach is not merely about making your website "fit" on a smaller screen; it's about crafting an experience that's easy, intuitive, and enjoyable for mobile users. Mobile-first design forces you to rethink how your website's content is structured, how elements are displayed, and how visitors interact with your site.

For example, on a small mobile screen, visitors won't have the luxury of scrolling through long paragraphs of text without losing interest. Therefore, mobile-first design encourages you to streamline your content and make sure that the most important information is front and center.

When you prioritize mobile users in your design process, you can ensure a smoother experience for all visitors, whether they're on a desktop or a smartphone.

Google also rewards mobile-friendly sites with higher rankings in search results, so optimizing for mobile isn't just good for your audience—it's good for your SEO as well.

Easy Ways to Make Your Site Mobile-Friendly

Making your website mobile-friendly doesn't require a complete redesign, but it does involve thoughtful adjustments that ensure it functions well on all devices.

Start by adopting a responsive design, which allows your website to adjust to different screen sizes automatically. With responsive design, your website's layout, images, and text will dynamically resize and reorganize themselves based on the device's screen dimensions, providing an optimal viewing experience no matter how the site is accessed.

One of the most important aspects of responsive design is ensuring that your images are properly sized for different screen resolutions. Large images that load quickly on a desktop can cause delays or appear distorted on smaller screens.

Using scalable vector graphics (SVGs) or compressed image formats can help maintain quality without slowing down your page load times.

Another essential element of mobile-friendliness is the simplification of menus and buttons. On a desktop, you have the luxury of more space to organize your navigation, but on mobile devices, real estate is limited.

Make sure your site's navigation is easy to use with a menu that's optimized for smaller screens. Many mobile-friendly sites utilize "hamburger" menus, which hide the navigation links behind a simple icon that opens up into a full menu when clicked.

Keep in mind that mobile users may be on the go, and they want information quickly. This means minimizing the amount of text and focusing on concise, easy-to-scan content.

Avoid clutter and prioritize the most important elements—clear headlines, short paragraphs, and easy-to-read buttons or links. For example, if your website contains a contact form, ensure it is simple and user-friendly, with input fields that are appropriately sized for a mobile device.

Interactive elements, like sliders, pop-ups, and forms, should also be tested for mobile use. Mobile screens are touch-sensitive, so elements that are designed for mouse clicks might not work as intended on mobile devices. Make sure buttons are large enough to be tapped easily and that any interactive content functions smoothly on smaller screens.

Finally, consider implementing touch gestures for mobile users. Gestures like swiping, pinching, and tapping are second nature to most smartphone users, and you can leverage them to improve navigation and interaction with your site. For example, implementing swipeable galleries or touch-activated buttons can make the experience more intuitive.

Navigation and Speed: Making Visitors Stay

While mobile optimization is essential, it's only one piece of the puzzle. Another critical factor in user experience is the ease with which visitors can navigate your site and the speed at which it loads.

If visitors struggle to find what they're looking for or your pages take too long to load, they will quickly bounce and look for a more seamless experience elsewhere.

Navigation is the map by which visitors explore your website. If your website's layout is confusing or difficult to navigate, users will become frustrated and leave. As mentioned, simplifying your navigation for mobile devices is a key first step.

However, it's also important to maintain logical organization and consistency across all devices. Make sure visitors can find your most important pages—like your About, Services, and Contact pages—within just a few clicks or taps.

Clarity and simplicity are vital. Overloaded menus or confusing page hierarchies can cause visitors to get lost. On mobile devices, where real estate is even more limited, every button, menu, and link should have a purpose and be clearly labeled. Visitors should know exactly where they are on your site and how to get to the next piece of information they need.

Equally important is page speed. Mobile users are often on the go, so they expect pages to load quickly. A delay of even a few seconds can significantly impact your bounce rate, which, in turn, can harm your site's search engine ranking.

To improve load times, optimize images, use proper caching techniques, and minimize the use of heavy

JavaScript or excessive plugins that can bog down your website.

Consider using tools like Google PageSpeed Insights to test your site's performance. This tool provides specific recommendations for improving load times, such as compressing images, eliminating render-blocking resources, and reducing server response time. These technical optimizations are critical for improving both mobile and desktop site performance.

In addition to speed, it's also important to ensure that your site remains accessible to users with different needs. This includes implementing features like adjustable text sizes, high contrast modes, and easy-to-read fonts. Accessibility features help ensure that your site is inclusive and provides a better user experience for all visitors, regardless of their circumstances.

Delivering a Seamless Mobile Experience

Optimizing for mobile isn't just about making sure your site fits on a small screen; it's about delivering an experience that feels as smooth, fast, and intuitive as possible. Mobile-first design, responsive layouts, optimized navigation, and fast load times are all components of a website that meets the needs of today's mobile users.

When you prioritize mobile optimization, you're ensuring that your site is accessible to the growing number of users who rely on smartphones to access the web.

But the work doesn't end there. Regularly testing your site's mobile functionality, gathering feedback from users, and staying up-to-date with design trends and technological advancements will help keep your website fresh and relevant.

The digital landscape is constantly evolving, and staying ahead of the curve ensures that your website remains a powerful, effective tool for your audience.

When you focus on mobile and user experience, you not only create a website that meets the expectations of modern visitors but also enhance your website's performance in ways that drive engagement and conversions. Your website isn't just a digital brochure—it's a dynamic platform that reflects your brand's commitment to quality, accessibility, and user satisfaction.

As you continue refining and optimizing your site, remember that every small improvement you make to the mobile experience will have a lasting impact on your site's success.

By ensuring your website looks great and functions seamlessly across devices, you're setting yourself up for long-term growth and lasting user engagement.

CHAPTER NINE

Basic SEO — Getting Found on Google

When it comes to launching a website, having a beautiful, well-functioning site is only part of the equation. No matter how appealing your content or design may be, if people can't find your website, it's all for naught. This is where search engine optimization (SEO) comes into play.

SEO is the practice of making your website more visible to search engines like Google, so that when people search for topics related to your business or niche, your site appears among the top results.

This chapter will introduce you to the basics of SEO, why it matters, and some simple techniques you can implement yourself to improve your site's visibility. We will also touch on how to set up Google

Analytics and Google Search Console to track your performance.

What Is SEO and Why It Matters

SEO, or Search Engine Optimization, is the process of enhancing your website in a way that helps it rank higher on search engines like Google. Simply put, it's the art and science of making sure that search engines can find and understand the content of your site, and deem it valuable enough to present to users searching for relevant terms.

Every time a person searches for something on Google, the search engine uses algorithms to sift through millions of web pages to find the most relevant results. Those results are ranked based on numerous factors such as relevance, trustworthiness, user experience, and content quality.

Understanding SEO is essential because the vast majority of website traffic comes from search engines. A high-ranking page on Google, for example, is far more likely to be clicked than a page buried on the fifth or sixth page of results. Without a solid SEO strategy, your website might remain invisible, regardless of how great your content is or how well-designed your website may be.

SEO isn't a one-time task but an ongoing process that evolves with search engine updates and trends. By following SEO best practices, you can steadily build your site's authority and trustworthiness, improving your chances of being found by users who are looking for exactly what you offer.

Simple On-Page SEO Techniques You Can Do Yourself

On-page SEO refers to all the things you can do directly on your website to help it rank higher in search engine results. Fortunately, many of these techniques are straightforward and can be done without any prior technical knowledge. One of the simplest and most impactful changes you can make is optimizing your website's content.

Begin with keywords. Keywords are the words or phrases that people type into search engines when they're looking for information. For example, if you're running a website that offers pet products, a keyword might be "best dog toys" or "affordable cat food." To optimize your content, you'll want to include relevant keywords in key areas such as your page titles, headers, and within the body of your text.

However, it's crucial to avoid keyword stuffing—filling your content with keywords in an unnatural way. Instead, focus on writing valuable, engaging content that naturally incorporates the keywords your audience is searching for.

Another important factor is meta descriptions. A meta description is a short summary of a webpage's content that appears in search engine results below the page title. While meta descriptions don't directly impact rankings, they can influence whether or not people click on your page. Craft compelling, relevant meta descriptions for each of your web pages to increase click-through rates.

Heading tags, such as H1, H2, and H3, are also crucial for on-page SEO. These tags help both search engines and readers understand the structure of your content. For example, the H1 tag should be used for your main title, and H2 or H3 tags should be used for subheadings. This structure makes your content easier to scan, and helps search engines know which topics are most important.

Furthermore, optimizing your images is a powerful yet often overlooked aspect of on-page SEO. Every image on your website should have an alt tag, which is a description of the image that helps search engines understand what the image is about.

This not only improves accessibility for people with visual impairments but also gives your images a better chance of appearing in Google's image search. Additionally, compressing your images to reduce their file size can improve page load times, which is an important ranking factor.

Internal linking is another simple yet effective strategy for SEO. By linking to other pages within your website, you help search engines understand the relationships between your pages and guide visitors to more valuable content.

Internal links also encourage visitors to spend more time on your site, reducing bounce rates and signaling to Google that your site is valuable and worth exploring.

Setting Up Google Analytics and Search Console

No SEO strategy is complete without the ability to track and measure your website's performance. That's where Google Analytics and Google Search Console are very useful. These powerful, free tools give you valuable insights into how your website is performing and how visitors are interacting with it.

Google Analytics allows you to track key metrics such as website traffic, user behavior, and conversions. With Analytics, you can see how many people are visiting your website, what pages they're looking at, how long they're staying, and whether they're taking actions like filling out a form or making a purchase.

This data helps you understand what's working on your website and what needs improvement. For example, if you notice that visitors are leaving your site quickly after visiting certain pages, it may signal that those pages need better content or a more intuitive design.

Google Analytics also provides information about where your traffic is coming from. You can see how many people are arriving from organic search (i.e., Google), social media, paid ads, or direct traffic. This breakdown can help you assess the effectiveness of your SEO efforts and determine which channels are driving the most traffic to your site.

Google Search Console, on the other hand, is focused specifically on how Google interacts with your website. With Search Console, you can monitor your site's performance in Google search results, track your rankings for various keywords, and identify any issues that might be preventing your pages from being indexed correctly.

It can also alert you to any potential technical issues on your website, such as broken links or slow-loading pages, that could negatively affect your SEO.

Setting up both Google Analytics and Search Console is relatively straightforward. For Analytics, you'll need to add a tracking code to your website's header. Once that's done, you can begin reviewing detailed reports about your site's performance.

For Search Console, you'll need to verify that you own the website, which can be done by adding a meta tag to your site's code or linking your domain to your Google account. Once verified, you'll be able to monitor your site's visibility in Google search results, submit sitemaps, and address any issues that arise.

CHAPTER TEN

Adding Extra Features (Without Coding!)

When you build a website, the journey doesn't end with a functional homepage and a few pages of content. To truly make your site engaging, user-friendly, and effective, you'll need to add extra features that enhance the overall experience.

The good news is that many of these enhancements can be achieved without writing a single line of code. With the right tools, you can integrate sophisticated functionalities such as contact forms, email newsletters, social media buttons, and even e-commerce capabilities—all through plugins and apps.

Installing Plugins and Apps

One of the easiest ways to extend the functionality of your website is through plugins and apps. These are software components designed to add specific features to your site without requiring complex coding. Whether you're using a website builder like WordPress, Wix, or Squarespace, plugins and apps are available to help you customize your site, improve performance, and add useful tools.

Installing plugins and apps typically involves selecting the tool you want, clicking "install," and activating it. For WordPress users, the process is incredibly straightforward. Within the WordPress dashboard, you can search for the plugin or app you want, install it with a click, and then activate it to start customizing your site.

These plugins cover a wide range of functionalities—from SEO optimization to social media sharing buttons, website security features, and everything in between.

It's important to remember that while plugins can add powerful features to your website, it's equally essential to keep your plugins updated. Outdated plugins may become vulnerable to security threats or simply stop working as intended. Always make sure to update your plugins regularly, and only install plugins from trusted sources to maintain the security and integrity of your site.

For website builders like Wix or Squarespace, adding extra features is just as simple. These platforms often have built-in apps or integrations that allow you to easily add functionality to your site, such as adding an event calendar, integrating payment systems, or embedding forms. The process of adding and managing these features is user-friendly and requires no technical skills.

Contact Forms, Newsletters, and Social Media Integration

When it comes to connecting with your website's visitors, contact forms and newsletters are essential tools. A contact form allows users to reach out to you directly from your site, whether they have questions, feedback, or inquiries about your services.

Integrating a contact form is typically as simple as installing a form plugin or using the built-in form builders available within your platform.

Most website builders provide easy-to-use templates for contact forms that require minimal customization. You can add fields such as name, email, phone number, and a message box to gather the information you need. You can also automate responses to thank visitors for reaching out or confirm that their message has been received.

Furthermore, by integrating your contact form with an email marketing tool like MailChimp or ConvertKit, you can automatically add people to your email list for future communications.

Building an email newsletter list is another powerful way to engage with your audience and drive traffic back to your website. Newsletters allow you to stay in touch with visitors, offer exclusive content, and keep them updated on new products or services. To integrate an email signup form, you can use dedicated newsletter plugins like MailChimp for WordPress or built-in features within Wix and Squarespace.

With these tools, visitors can easily subscribe to your newsletter, and you can automate the process of sending regular updates to your subscribers.

Social media integration is another valuable feature for any website. By connecting your website to social media platforms like Facebook, Twitter, Instagram, or LinkedIn, you provide visitors with a seamless way to share your content, products, and services.

Integrating social media buttons can be done through simple plugins or built-in features, and they give your visitors the ability to like, share, or follow your social media profiles directly from your site.

This kind of integration not only boosts your visibility on social platforms but also enhances your brand's credibility and trustworthiness. Visitors who see your social media activity will be more likely to engage with your business, and sharing your content on social media can attract more visitors to your website. Many social media plugins also allow you to display your social media feeds directly on your website, making it easier for users to interact with your brand.

E-Commerce Basics: Setting Up a Simple Online Store (Optional)

For those who are looking to turn their website into an online store, adding e-commerce functionality is easier than ever—no coding required. Whether you're selling physical products, digital downloads, or services, there are a variety of tools available that make setting up an online store a seamless process.

For WordPress users, one of the most popular tools for adding e-commerce features is WooCommerce, a plugin that transforms your website into a fully functional online store.

WooCommerce allows you to add product listings, set up payment gateways (such as PayPal or Stripe), and manage orders—all from within your WordPress dashboard. It's highly customizable, so you can choose from a wide range of themes, add-ons, and extensions to tailor your store to your brand.

On platforms like Wix and Squarespace, adding e-commerce features is just as simple. Both offer integrated e-commerce tools that allow you to add an online store with ease.

With Wix, for example, you can use their Wix Stores feature to create a storefront, manage inventory, and process payments. Squarespace also offers e-commerce templates that allow you to sell products, track orders, and accept payments through a variety of methods.

Setting up your store involves adding product images, descriptions, and pricing details. You'll also need to choose your payment methods. Most e-commerce tools support a wide range of payment gateways, so you can choose the one that works best for you and your customers.

In addition to payments, you'll also want to ensure that your shipping and tax settings are configured correctly to avoid any confusion for your customers. Both Wix and Squarespace make this process intuitive, with built-in tools that allow you to set shipping rates and manage taxes based on your location and the products you're selling.

The key to a successful online store is not just about having an e-commerce solution, but also providing a smooth, professional user experience. High-quality product images, clear product descriptions, and easy navigation are essential to encouraging visitors to make a purchase.

Many e-commerce platforms also offer tools to help you track sales, offer discounts, and manage customer service, giving you everything you need to run an online business efficiently.

CHAPTER ELEVEN

Testing, Troubleshooting, and Launching

After weeks, or perhaps months, of designing, building, and refining your website, the time has finally arrived to launch it to the public. But before you hit that "publish" button and share your hard work with the world, it's essential to ensure that everything functions seamlessly. Testing and troubleshooting are critical steps in the website creation process.

A well-launched website can make an immediate impact, but a website with errors or slow loading times can result in frustrated visitors and lost opportunities. In this chapter, we'll explore how to conduct final testing, identify and fix potential problems, and confidently launch your website to the world.

Final Pre-Launch Checklist

Before you make your website live, it's important to go through a comprehensive pre-launch checklist. This is your opportunity to ensure that every aspect of your website works as intended, from the design and user experience to its technical performance. Think of it as your last line of defense against launching a site with errors that could affect its effectiveness.

Start by thoroughly reviewing all your content. Ensure that text is free from typos, broken links are repaired, and images and videos load properly. Also, check that every page displays correctly on different devices and browsers.

You'd be surprised at how sometimes even small layout issues, like text that overlaps or buttons that don't align correctly, can negatively impact a visitor's perception of your website. Check that the mobile version of your site is user-friendly, as more people browse the web on mobile devices than ever before.

Next, test all your forms and buttons. Whether you have a contact form, a newsletter signup, or a purchase button, ensure these elements work smoothly. Submitting a test message through the contact form or completing a test purchase through your e-commerce platform will help you verify that the forms are functioning as they should.

It's crucial to ensure these features work not only for your convenience but also to avoid frustrating users who may want to reach out or make a purchase.

Another important step in your pre-launch process is checking your website's loading speed. A slow website can be a major deterrent to visitors. Test how quickly your website loads on various devices and internet connections.

Tools like Google PageSpeed Insights or GTmetrix can help analyze your site's speed and offer suggestions for improvement. Compressing images, minimizing unnecessary scripts, and using a content delivery network (CDN) can all help to boost your site's performance.

In addition, make sure all your SEO elements are in place. Review your meta titles and descriptions for each page, ensuring they are concise and accurate. Double-check that your website has the necessary headers and that images are tagged with descriptive alt text.

These SEO basics will help ensure your site is indexed properly by search engines, which can help drive traffic to your site post-launch.

Lastly, confirm that all essential integrations are set up and working. If you're using tools like Google Analytics to track website traffic or integrating email marketing services, now is the time to ensure they are properly configured.

Testing these integrations will save you from troubleshooting later on, allowing you to track performance data and continue to improve your site after launch.

Common Mistakes to Avoid

Even experienced web developers make mistakes when launching a website. However, these errors can be easily avoided with careful planning and attention to detail.

One common mistake that many new website owners make is forgetting to back up their website before launching. While this might seem like a simple step, it's crucial to create a backup of your site before making it public. If something goes wrong after launch—whether it's a failed plugin installation or an accidental deletion of key content—you can restore your site without losing everything you've worked for.

Another common mistake is ignoring mobile optimization. A website that looks great on a desktop but is difficult to navigate on a mobile device can drive users away. It's essential to ensure that your website is responsive, meaning it automatically adjusts to fit different screen sizes. Take the time to test how your website appears on smartphones and tablets, and make adjustments as needed to improve the user experience.

Many website owners also overlook the importance of testing their website's forms. Whether it's a contact form, a checkout process for an online store, or a newsletter sign-up form, these are some of the most vital parts of your website.

If a form doesn't work correctly, users may become frustrated and leave your site without completing the desired action. Test all forms and interactive elements to ensure they're easy to use and fully functional.

Another mistake often made by first-time website owners is neglecting the privacy and security of their visitors. In today's world, data security is of utmost importance. Make sure your website has an SSL certificate installed.

This secures the connection between your website and visitors, encrypting sensitive information such as login details and payment information. SSL certification also boosts your site's SEO ranking, as Google considers SSL a ranking factor. Don't skip this step—it's essential for building trust with your audience and ensuring their data is safe.

Lastly, many people forget to proofread their content before going live. It might seem trivial, but misspellings or grammatical errors on your website can make you look unprofessional and damage your credibility.

Take the time to read through all of your text before launching, or even ask someone else to review it for you. Clean, polished content can go a long way in presenting a professional image to your visitors.

Going Live With Confidence

Once you've completed your final checklist and addressed any potential issues, it's time to go live with your website. This moment can be both exciting and nerve-wracking, but with thorough preparation, you can approach it with confidence. Remember, your website is an ongoing project. While the launch is a major milestone, it doesn't mark the end of your work. In fact, the launch is just the beginning of an ongoing process of improvement, monitoring, and growth.

When you hit the "publish" button and make your website live, take a moment to celebrate. You've put in the effort, learned a ton of new skills, and created something unique and valuable.

After the launch, focus on promoting your website. Share it on social media, send an email to your contacts, and consider running digital ads to drive traffic. The goal at this point is to get your website in front of as many people as possible to start generating interest and engagement.

Once the site goes live, keep monitoring its performance. Use Google Analytics to track website traffic and user behavior. This data can provide valuable insights into how visitors are interacting with your site and where improvements can be made. Over time, you can tweak your site based on user feedback and analytical data, ensuring it stays relevant, functional, and effective.

CHAPTER TWELVE

Maintaining and Growing Your Website

Creating a website is just the beginning of an ongoing journey. Once your site is live and visitors begin to interact with it, your role as a website owner evolves. The key to sustaining a successful website lies not only in its initial design and launch but in how well you maintain and grow it over time.

Maintaining and growing your website ensures that it continues to serve your audience effectively, reflect your brand's evolving identity, and adapt to technological changes and trends.

Updating Your Site Regularly

The digital landscape is constantly changing. New technologies, design trends, and user preferences emerge every day. A website that stays static risks becoming outdated, which can lead to decreased traffic and engagement. One of the most important tasks you'll need to perform after launching your site is regularly updating its content, design, and features. Consistent updates show your visitors that you are actively maintaining your site, and this can increase trust and credibility in your brand.

Content is at the heart of every website, and keeping it fresh and relevant is essential for attracting repeat visitors. Whether you run a blog, offer services, or sell products, updating your site regularly with new articles, products, or promotions keeps your audience engaged and encourages them to return.

For example, if you're running a blog, aim to post new articles on a consistent schedule. If you're managing an e-commerce site, regularly refresh your product offerings and descriptions to reflect new trends, stock updates, or seasonal changes.

Another key area to update is your website's technology and design. While your website might look great when it first launches, user preferences and technology tend to shift over time. Keeping your site modern involves updating its design elements, user interface, and functionality.

Simple changes, such as refreshing your color scheme, reorganizing navigation menus for ease of use, or implementing new features (like interactive galleries or advanced search functions), can breathe new life into your website. Additionally, web design trends change, so ensuring your site's aesthetics align with current standards helps improve the user experience.

Backups and Basic Security Tips

Maintaining a website is not just about keeping it fresh and functional; it's also about protecting it from unexpected disruptions. Websites, especially those that handle sensitive data, can become targets for cyberattacks, data breaches, and technical failures. Regular backups and solid security measures are essential in keeping your website safe and secure.

Start by implementing a regular backup routine. No matter how reliable your hosting provider is, unexpected issues such as server crashes, hacking attempts, or even simple human errors can cause data loss. Backup tools can automate the process, ensuring that you always have a recent version of your site stored securely, ready to be restored if needed.

Depending on your platform, there are various plugins and services that offer automatic backups at set intervals, saving you from having to manually back up your website. Regular backups will give you peace of mind, knowing that if anything goes wrong, you can restore your website to its previous state without significant downtime or loss of content.

Alongside backups, basic website security should be a top priority. Hackers are constantly looking for vulnerabilities, and if your website isn't properly secured, it may be vulnerable to attacks that could compromise user data or cause your site to go offline. One of the simplest ways to improve your website's security is by installing an SSL certificate. SSL (Secure Sockets Layer) ensures that the data exchanged between your site and your visitors is encrypted and secure, protecting sensitive information like credit card details or login credentials.

Additionally, Google rewards websites with SSL certificates by ranking them higher in search results, improving your SEO and credibility.

Other basic security measures include using strong, unique passwords for your website and admin accounts. A good password management tool can help you keep track of your login details without the need to remember every password. Regularly updating your platform, plugins, and themes is also vital, as these updates often contain security patches that fix vulnerabilities.

Using secure hosting providers and enabling two-factor authentication for your accounts adds an extra layer of security to protect against potential breaches.

By taking proactive steps to ensure your site's security and implementing regular backups, you safeguard both your content and the trust of your visitors. A secure website not only provides peace of mind but also builds credibility with your audience, which is critical for maintaining long-term success.

Easy Ways to Keep Improving Your Website

A website that isn't continually improved can quickly fall behind in terms of performance, usability, and visitor engagement. Fortunately, there are several straightforward ways to keep improving your website over time. One of the best approaches is to focus on collecting and analyzing user feedback.

Your website's visitors are a valuable source of information about what's working and what isn't. Consider implementing surveys, feedback forms, or even tracking engagement metrics through Google Analytics to understand how users are interacting with your site.

Based on the feedback you receive, you can make data-driven decisions to enhance your website. For instance, if visitors consistently point out that your site's navigation is confusing, you can reorganize your menu or simplify the layout.

If you find that users are dropping off during the checkout process on your e-commerce site, you can streamline the steps to make it more intuitive. Over time, these small adjustments can add up to significant improvements in user experience and satisfaction.

Another great way to continuously improve your site is through A/B testing. A/B testing allows you to test two versions of a page or element to see which one performs better in terms of user engagement or conversions.

For example, you might test two different headlines on your homepage or two variations of a call-to-action button. By experimenting with different elements and analyzing the results, you can optimize your website's performance and ensure that it's effectively meeting its goals.

As you grow and learn more about your audience, it's important to refine your website's content. Regularly updating your blog or adding new content that addresses your audience's needs will not only keep your site fresh but will also improve your SEO ranking.

Engaging, high-quality content is one of the most effective ways to attract organic traffic, and as your website evolves, you can tailor your content to reflect the interests and questions of your target audience.

Another key area for improvement is website speed. Over time, as you add new content, features, and media to your site, it can slow down. A slow website can negatively impact user experience and even harm your SEO rankings.

You can improve site speed by optimizing images, reducing unnecessary plugins, and using tools like caching and content delivery networks (CDNs).

Regularly testing and optimizing for speed will help keep your website running efficiently and provide a better experience for visitors.

Finally, staying current with SEO best practices is essential for growing your website's visibility. Search engine optimization is an ongoing process, and as search engine algorithms evolve, so should your SEO strategy.

Monitor your rankings and adjust your content, keywords, and on-page SEO tactics accordingly. Keeping your website optimized for search engines is crucial to attracting new visitors and staying competitive in the digital landscape.

CONCLUSION

Congratulations! You've now successfully built your website from the ground up, launched it to the world, and navigated through the complexities of creating an online presence. What you've accomplished is an incredible feat, and with the right mindset and continuous effort, you're equipped to make your website thrive in an ever-evolving digital world.

Creating a website may seem like a daunting task, especially if you've never written a line of code, but as you've seen throughout this book, it's entirely possible to build something beautiful, functional, and impactful without any technical expertise. From setting up your domain and choosing the perfect platform to designing your site, crafting compelling content, and optimizing it for mobile, you now have the knowledge and tools necessary to build a lasting online presence.

But the work doesn't stop here. Websites require constant attention and nurturing. You'll need to keep your content fresh, optimize for better performance, monitor your security, and grow your brand to stay ahead of the competition. It's the ongoing effort that will turn your website into a powerful tool that serves your audience and achieves your goals.

As you move forward, keep in mind that your website is more than just a digital space; it's a reflection of you, your values, and the message you want to share with the world. Whether you're launching a blog, showcasing your portfolio, starting an e-commerce store, or simply sharing your passion, every aspect of your website should reflect your unique identity and purpose.

The digital world is ever-changing, and so should your website. As you continue to learn, grow, and adapt, your website will evolve with you. Embrace the challenges, celebrate the successes, and keep moving forward with confidence.

Thank you for taking this journey with me. Now, it's time for you to take your website to new heights.

Your audience is waiting – go ahead and show them what you've built. The world is yours to explore.

www.ingramcontent.com/pod-product-compliance
Lightning Source LLC
LaVergne TN
LVHW022353060326
832902LV00022B/4423